For Eva

All the best

Mike Harding

1996

POETRY ORIGINALS

Buns for the Elephants

Other Poetry Originals

Grandad's Seagulls *Ted Walker*
The Magnificent Callisto *Gerard Benson*
Nearly Thirteen *Jan Dean*
Two's Company *Jackie Kay*

SERIES EDITOR: ANNE HARVEY

POETRY ORIGINALS

Buns for the Elephants

by Mike Harding

Illustrated by Anna Leplar

VIKING

VIKING

Published by the Penguin Group
Penguin Books Ltd, 27 Wrights Lane, London W8 5TZ, England
Penguin Books USA Inc., 375 Hudson Street, New York, New York 10014, USA
Penguin Books Australia Ltd, Ringwood, Victoria, Australia
Penguin Books Canada Ltd, 10 Alcorn Avenue, Toronto, Ontario, Canada M4V 3B2
Penguin Books (NZ) Ltd, 182–90 Wairau Road, Auckland 10, New Zealand

Penguin Books Ltd, Registered Offices: Harmondsworth, Middlesex, England

First published 1995
1 3 5 7 9 10 8 6 4 2

Text copyright © Mike Harding, 1995
Illustrations copyright © Anna Leplar, 1995

The poem 'Mushycat' was previously published in
Daddy Edgar's Pools, Peterloo Poets, 1992

The moral right of the author has been asserted

All rights reserved.
Without limiting the rights under copyright reserved above,
no part of this publication may be reproduced, stored in or introduced into a
retrieval system, or transmitted, in any form or by any means (electronic,
mechanical, photocopying, recording or otherwise), without the prior written
permission of both the copyright owner and the above publisher of this book

Filmset in Monotype Palatino by Selwood Systems, Midsomer Norton

Made and printed in Great Britain by Butler & Tanner Ltd, Frome and London

A CIP catalogue record for this book is available from the British Library

ISBN 0–670–85987–7

Contents

Introduction 7

The Singing Street 11

Good Morning, Morning 13
A Day It Is 15
Ants 16
Mushycat 18
Guy Fawkes Night 20
Frost Picture 22
Christmas Market 23
My Grandfather's Violin 24
For Carlo 26
In a Desk 28
School Bully 30
Junior School Teacher 32
Buns for the Elephants 34
The Bike 37
The Dump 38
Bobby Swings 39

The Road to Beyond 41

The Son of the King of Nowhere 43
What of the Night? 45
Lucky Legs 46

Jimmy Spoons   48
The Sally-dosser Man   50
Sheffield With Roses   52
Train by Skerries   53
Merman   54

Mapmaking   55

Alphabet   57
Village Wedding   58
After the Wedding   61
Wind and the Angries   62
The Song of the Flute   66
The Heroic Clouds   67
Curtains   68
Swallows   70
Autumn Dentdale   72
Lune Sun   73
Diggers   74
Mapmakers   76
Paper Boats   77

Index of First Lines   79

Introduction

Shakespeare's famous line 'One man in his time plays many parts' could well apply to Mike Harding, one of the most versatile men I have ever met. Ask someone, 'Do you know Mike Harding?' and the answer could be: 'Oh, you mean the comedian, don't you?' or 'Yes...he's a travel writer and photographer, isn't he?' or 'Of course I know him...the singer they used to call the Rochdale Cowboy!' And all those replies are right. But I know him best as a poet whose work I discovered when his adult collection *Daddy Edgar's Pools* was published in 1992; poems rich in imagery and use of language that told of real life, real people, real places. I knew at once that I wanted him to write for POETRY ORIGINALS, and his response was immediate and enthusiastic. Enthusiasm, as you'll discover, is a strong part of his character.

In January 1994 we met. It was his wife, Pat, who arranged my visit – Pat, who makes sure that appointments are kept, deadlines met, bookings confirmed, visitors welcomed, and...and...Shakespeare might have added, 'One *woman* in her time plays many parts'! The two are a team. Pat's wit, expertise and organization must be a great loss to the teaching profession.

The view from the windows of the Hardings' sixteenth-century Yorkshire cottage – of sky and mountain peaks – took my Londoner's breath away. To the north are the Howgill Fells; to the south, Whernside; one of the most beautiful and dramatic parts of the Dales. The cottage is a hive of activity, but relaxed and welcoming too; I felt at home at once among books and pictures and ornaments;

photographs of Pat and Mike's daughters, Sarah and Emma, and nephews and nieces. Colours and shapes and textures caught my eye, and in Mike's study is a most magnificent, large, heavy wood chair, carved for him by a local craftsman.

Work spills from the cottage down a track to the studio, once a barn. Old and new materials, wood and stone, blend to make a workplace that is both attractive and businesslike. Being so untidy myself, I envied the cataloguing and organization of tapes and videos, books and photographic slides; everything neatly in place. Colour streamed through a stained-glass window, a design of moon, fields and winding lane. The eyes of a carved green man followed me round the space.

On one wall are fascinating masks from many countries, collected on Mike's travels: Tibet, Mexico, Japan, Africa, North America and Italy. There are all kinds of musical instruments: guitars, banjos, mandolins; equipment for electronic music. Mike is a self-taught musician; he can't read music, but composes and plays. The close relationship of musician and instrument is brought out in the poem 'The Song of the Flute':

> Blow a breath into me, man...
> Come lip to lip and let us, lovers, kiss.

It doesn't take long to discover that there's not much Mike won't try his hand at and master; he thrives on change and challenge.

Although I was there to discuss the proposed book, our talk turned, inevitably, to the story of Mike's life. He was born in Crumpsall, Manchester, in 1944, into a working-class Irish-Catholic family. The memories of those post-war years colour his writing. He missed the war, but was deeply affected by it: his father was killed in a bombing mission before Mike was born.

Books, stories and poems were important from the beginning. An early favourite was Robert Louis Stevenson's *A Child's Garden of Verses*, read to him by his mother. Later, other poems caught his imagination: 'The Listeners' by Walter de la Mare, stirring ballads by Kipling, 'The Highwayman' by Alfred Noyes, and Henry Newbolt's 'The Fighting Téméraire'. In his teens came the First World War poets, and then Dylan Thomas, T.S. Eliot, Philip Larkin, Seamus Heaney. Like many writers, it was encouragement from a fine English teacher – in Mike's case Father 'Foxy' Reynolds from St Bede's School, Manchester – that sparked off an interest in literature. The spark grew and led to total commitment.

Before going to university and taking a degree in Education Mike worked at a variety of jobs: dustman, bus-conductor, road-digger, bookshop assistant and boiler-scaler. And there was always music in his life. In the sixties he played in skiffle groups and rock-and-roll bands, and has happy memories of sharing the bill at various venues with the Beatles, Gerry and the Pacemakers, the Hollies and the Mindbenders. He has many LPs and singles where he accompanies his own folk-songs and lyrics.

During a gig with the Edison Bell Spasm Band in 1967, there was a sudden awkward pause. Undaunted, Mike jumped in with a few jokes. These went down well and the patter became part of the act. When he ran out of jokes he had an endless store of real-life tales to tell. He has played and performed in pubs and folk clubs, as well as on TV and in theatres. Not long ago he played his first professional acting part, as Vladimir in Samuel Beckett's offbeat, poetic play, *Waiting for Godot*. I wish I'd seen him.

He's a good actor. Last Easter, I turned on my television and there was Mike playing an innkeeper in a monologue about the Last Supper. Needless to say, he had also written the script. Another time, there he was, on the small screen, hosting an educational programme.

As well as his writing, music and performing there's a very different side to Mike's life – his great love of, and concern for, the countryside. He is Vice-President of the Ramblers Association and a Fellow of the Royal Geographic Society, in constant demand to give talks on the environment and ecology. Walking in England and abroad, and becoming an expert at photography, has led to several books that include *Walking the Peak and Pennines*, *Walking the Dales* and *Footloose in the Himalaya*.

With so many memories to draw on it's no wonder that Mike Harding's poems are powerful and perceptive. He cares passionately about the tools of language; understands the fine line between humour and sadness, comedy and tragedy. Poetry, he says, is one way to explore the mystery of life. Through these poems you will share some of the characters he has known – his grandfather, the sally-dosser man and Jimmy Spoons – and become part of the weathers and landscapes of his life.

ANNE HARVEY

PS The day after I'd written this I went into a bookshop and there on the 'new books' table was a collection of short stories by Mike Harding. I phoned to congratulate him – too late! – he was already off on a walking tour of Western Ireland, collecting ideas and photographs for his next travel book.

The Singing Street

Good Morning, Morning

I was up in the morning with nothing to do,
Ran down the street, got a hole in my shoe,
The sun was on the cobbles, I heard all the kids,
Cats sleeping quiet on the warm dustbin lids,
And they all said: *Good morning, morning.*

Up through the park then to Paradise Hill,
Where Time stands on tiptoe when the
                                  roundabout's still,
Dogs chasing paper and kids calling names
At the parkies who chase them and spoil all their
                                           games,
And they all said: *Good morning, morning.*

Morning wakes to the smell of bread
From bakehouse windowpanes,
The sound of traffic growling through the town,
The rattling of the trains,
The smell of smoky bacon and hot sweet tea,
The sound of a playground full of kids.

Faces at windows, fingers at doors,
Seagulls that sing and buses that snore,
Schoolgirls with satchels and wind-blown hair,
Red-faced policemen and old ladies who stare,
And they all said: *Good morning, morning.*

A sea full of chimneys points to the sky,
Down the street women hang washing on lines,
Grannies with cushions are sat on their steps,

And grandads with pipes and scarves round
                                           their necks,
And they all said: *Good morning, morning.*

Down through the market where work is all done,
The iron and glass shine out warm in the sun,
Wind blows the papers and scraps down the street
And ties them in tangles round everyone's feet,
And they all said: *Good morning, morning.*

Down to the river to watch the world pass,
Faces that hurry like sand through a glass
Into their city their wages to earn,
And me without a penny but a million words to
                                               burn,
And they all said: *Good morning, morning.*

A Day It Is

A day it is that fingers its way
Through the crack in the curtains, the day
Nudging us, opening our eyes as the kids did
Long years back asking, *Are you awake, Daddy,*

Mummy? Such a day it is that toast
And coffee breathe through the warming house
And the summer's morning is outside
Telling us to hurry up, not to lie

Such sluggards. And we rise and walk the fell
And drink from streams and larks tell
The hot air their business, and we
Wander back as long light streaks

And licks the crag in a dying blaze
And I imagine that we are in love again, it is
                                        such a day.

Ants

I saw them as I lay beside the pools
Strung through the croft beneath the tip.
Fly boatmen skiffed across the rusty scum
And the air was thick and heavy with the stink
Of oil and rust, slag and tar. I dozed a while,
A Gulliver of the dump.

With half an eye, I saw them, was aware
Of something moving dark across the path,
Slick oil or varnish; then I made out,
Bit by bit, their shape.

In relentless column they scurried from the
                                          grass,
Scuttled and scraped across the cinders
And disappeared into the thin, pale shoots
Of moss that forested the other side.

I watched all afternoon until the queen,
Held and pushed by urgent ministers,
Scrabbled heavily across the gritty plains.

Then it was dusk, and I saw the last
Foot-soldiers in frantic file tumbling
Across the clinker on the path,
Clutching their precious eggs tight in their jaws;
While down below the lights came on in the
                                                  town,
The hurrying workers headed home
And traffic droned towards the quiet zones.

Then I thought of ants and wondered at the
                                                  knowledge
And the force that pushed them on
To jumble them across the path that day,
Carrying their children out before them, held
Like white stars in the frantic, falling dusk.

Mushycat

Had a cat, Mushycat,
Old before I was born,
Lived greyly another ten years after that,
A bony cushion cuffed off chairs.

Scruffy cat,
Dawdled on rooftops rimed by the frosty moon,
Rubbed about the chimneys with his whiskers
                                                           cocked

And, like a black knight,
Mated and went his way.

Lame cat,
Lost eight of his nine lives
Fighting coal-carts, buses and whippets
And disappeared to lose the ninth
One Christmas Day.
Found him,

Mushycat,
Stiff cat, a starched muff,
Cardboard model bogus cat,
Not our cat, flesh and fur cat, hob corner cat,
Steal the meat cat, trip my gran cat.

But it was him cat;
Scarred nose from Corkett's dog,
Ear ripped in a tom-fight,
Tail kinked in a careless kitchen door,
Legs all crooked and gangly,
And the fur half on, half off.

Dead Cat,
Our cat, Mushycat,
Lay, wide-eyed and grinning at death,
The hero-warrior of my tenth year,
Stiff as a full stocking in the Christmas snow.

Guy Fawkes Night

There was no walking then, only running
As across the still pool of the sky, fire foiled
Then fleshed and crumbled and we pushed,
                                      stumbled
Dizzy with excitement up the entry backs,
As a rocket bloomed on the black night

And multiplied in all the darkened windows of
The row. At street end flames whipped upwards
                                                  and
Licked at a frosty shaking moon. About the fire
A clump of stumpy figures cawed and called
With every rocket spurt and we fresh back
From benediction watched our guy sat on
Ma Hughes's soaking armchair that now
                                                  steamed
And clouded as a hail of sparks wept comets
Out to space swirling red snow, falling
On a bruised sky, curling about the moon,
Whisping around the people, dying paraclete.

Then all our street cheered as the guy
Caught flame, his legs and one arm first and
                                                  then
The waistcoat with the bangers in went off
And his eyes stared out unseeing at the plain
Of slates and chimneys, till the string
That held his head on was burnt through
And off it fell as a drunken voice in the
Crowd called out over the crackling flames,
They should've burned the bleedin' Pope
As well! and I watched dully, as a half-dud
Rocket spat into the sky and fluttered
Dimly on a night that suddenly was becoming
                                                  cold.

Frost Picture

The frost curled fat fine flowers of ice about
The privet stalks and mustered up a host
Of snowy-sworded armies in the grass.
Where the milkman's horse drew clouds of
                              steamy breath
The smell of bran and husk hung in the Saturday
                                            air.
A morning full of kids, school-free, brushed
                                            white
Dust off gate-tops with burning hands; then Bob
The milkman gave us rides slung on his cart
And rattled and jiggled us like empty bottles
                                            over
The crooked brew cobbles; between my legs, the
                                            icy
Setts spun past, the streets of childhood ran.

And now, a picture locked in ice, waits in its
                                            glass ball,
A snow-scene waiting for some word or sound
To shake again the Saturday morning world.

sett: paving-stone

Christmas Market

Tall, white-haired in her widow's black,
My Nanna took me, balaclava'd from the cold,
To where stalls shimmered in a splash of gold,
Buttery light from wind-twitched lamps and all
The Christmas hoards were heaped above my eyes,
A shrill cascade of tinsel set to fall
In a sea of shivering colours on the frosty
Foot-pocked earth. I smelt the roasted nuts,
Drank heavy sarsaparilla in thick glasses far
Too hot to hold and chewed a liquorice root
That turned into a soggy yellow brush. The man
Who wound the barrel-organ let me turn
The handle and I jangled out a tune –
And 'Lily of Laguna' spangled out into the still
                                                        night air
To go on spinning through the turning years.

Then we walked home. I clutched a bright tin car
With half-men painted on the windows, chewed
                                                        a sweet
And held my Nanna's hand as she warmed mine,
One glove lost turning out the chattering music.
And I looked up at the circus of the stars
That spread across the city and our street
Coated with a Christmas-cake layer of frost,
And nobody under all those stars I thought
Was a half of a half of a half as happy as me.

sarsaparilla: extract of dried roots, used as a tonic

My Grandfather's Violin

My grandfather played a fiddle
In the yard, with the end of his gloves
Cut off for his fingers to slide on
The gut. He played to the stars
And the neighbours in their dark,
Still-as-night houses,
And his relatives on planets
Reeling and ploughing through space.
And his long high notes cut amongst the
                              worlds –
And oh his skullcap!
And his head on one side
And his stories of battles in the sky!
And the light from the kitchen,
Spilt on the dustbin.
And my grandfather played his fiddle,
Tapped his feet on the step
And the moon jigged
And the stars sang

And the old man laughed, like the little dog
Watching the cow.

Not long after, he died,
Left his fiddle behind,
But the strings broke and the bow went slack.
Then when I was older in my turn
I gave the children the fiddle,
To play with in the snow.
And they built a snow fiddler
Fat, with cob o' coal eyes and a carroty nose
An old skull cap and stubby fingers.
And they gave it my grandfather's fiddle,
Stuck it under his chin.

Standing in the street under the gas-lamp,
A cold white man in the wind-fluted night,
A starry sky, a blustery light,
The snowman clutched his fiddle
And the ice fell in the scrolled holes
And all about was silence.

And then the snowman winked
One of his cob o' coal eyes
And there in the gaslight my snow-fiddler
Grandfather played, fingers sliding on the icy
                      strings,
'Shoe the Donkey' and 'Lanigan's Ball',
Throwing the wild notes out like upward-falling
                      snow
And the world, moon and houses, snowman and
                      lamp
Swung round with a laugh and a shout.

For Carlo

Every Sunday in summer he came in his van
And the kids all shouted, *Here's Carlo the ice-*
cream man!
Banging on doors as the van stopped and the
bell rang
And dads in armchairs woke up as the kids sang:

Hey, Mam, give us some money for Carlo,
Hey, Mam, give us some please before he goes.

He's got raspberry sauce, he tells us it's
elephant's blood;
I don't think it is, but, Mam, it tastes real good.
He's got wafers, cornets, ninety-niners and twists,
Oh, get your purse, Mam. Come on, Mam, get it
quick.

Hey, Mam, give us some money for Carlo,
Hey, Mam, give us some please before he goes.

Every year when the Whitsun Procession came round
He'd walk with all the other Italians in town;
He carried the madonna and gave us all a big smile
As the band played and the kids all cheered and went wild.

Hey, Mam, give us some money for Carlo,
Hey, Mam, give us some please before he goes.

And now on summer Sundays I take my own kids
And we walk down that old street where I used to live.
I sit down in my dad's old chair in the house,
The bell rings and the kids come in and all shout:

Hey, Dad, give us some money for Carlo,
Hey, Dad, give us it quick before he goes.
Hey, Dad, hurry up, don't be so slow,
Hey, Dad ...

In a Desk

In a desk he is caged,
Lulled uneasy by the teacher's barren song,
Locked from the sun, wind and rain.
Savaged by giants with gummed paper flowers,
He sits and feels the hours stop and spatter
With each nib split on the page,
And the day, his life, crawl by
With legs of twisting words.
So he leans on the desktop, sticky with milk and
                                                names,
And watches clouds outside the small high
                                                window
Map seas and foreign lands upon the windy sky.

Then he, a boy, becomes a bird,
Creeps through a crack in the door,
Out into the playground where,
Clear and mad it takes to the air,
Circling above the chimneys and the cranes,
The river and slate roofs, far into the sky's
Blue bowl to bunch and batter about the
                                                heavens.
Curling round the moon and stars he sits,
A giant bird, with a face as bright as the sun,
Pecking clauses and theorems from its feathers.

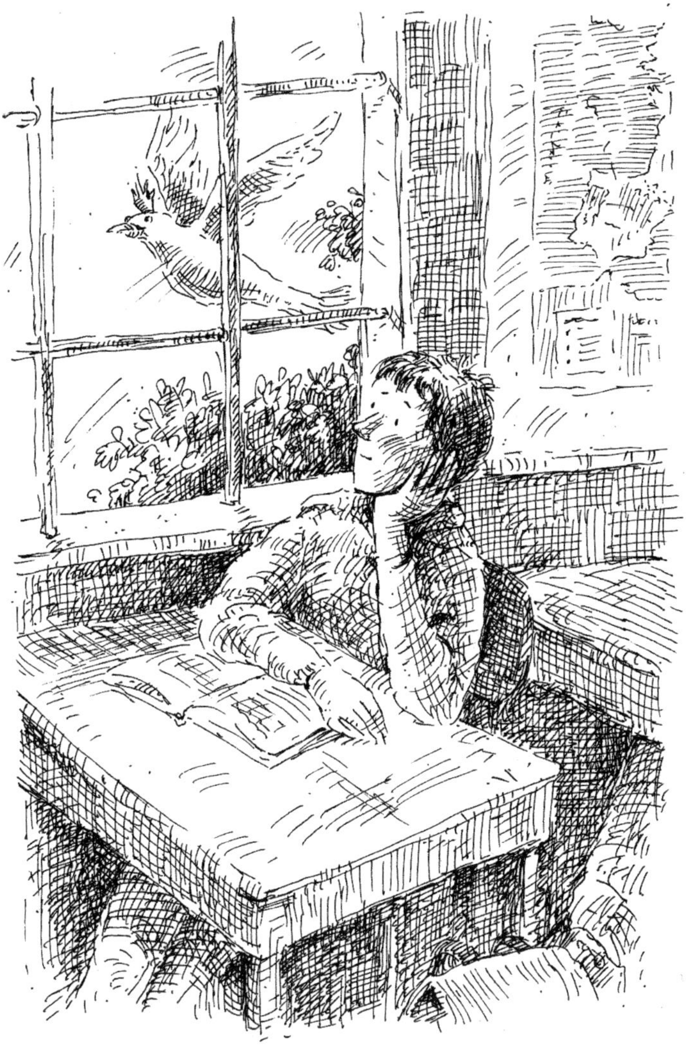

School Bully

Give in! your classmates said. *Give in!* – sharing
Your pain almost – as his knee sent glass
Slivers burning like black
Stars up
Your spine, and very close to your watering eye,
The many-sided worlds of grit
Shone in the playtime sun.
As he held you
Face down
Hard on the ground, you heard the skipping,
                                           wall-
Ball-bouncing voices that seemed now
So far from this mad world
Behind the bike
Shed. *No!*
You said to the urgent voices that
Were fearful of this lock, this jam of wills.

Yet somehow pain and fear
Went far away
And joined
The other little voices in the sun;
And as his face came closer and
You smelt his foul tobacco-
Stained breath hit
You like
An old, sad room, full of dark secrets, then
You knew you'd won, and as his hands
Like hard white spiders searched
You for a door
To let
More pain come crashing in, you smiled through
....tears,

Sensing his awful fear and loss
As, eternities away, the bell tolled.

Junior School Teacher

Your screaming sent the spiders to their holes
And brought the trembling class nose-down,
Blind inches from the page, a harvest field
Of scribbling, dry-nibbed pens. We daren't look
                                    up
To where your face twitched, as a thousand
                                devils flashed
Across your dark sky and the classroom shook
And shuddered. And we wondered, knowing
                                  nothing
That we'd done could call that black night in –
Not John even, with his bad teeth and harelip,
Or Mavis with her stutter and white eye
Could have tumbled you into that deep black
                                  pit.
And then you stopped and we looked up and
                                  saw
The shaking hands, the needle eyes, the thin
Pale crust of spittle starting to rime your lips,
                                  and heard
A laughing cry like the mad wind of a forgotten
                                  world.

And when years later word got round they'd
                                        locked
You up after you'd run naked round the school,
Shouting nonsense at the lupins in the priest's
Garden, I wondered what had happened to your
                                              mind:
What maggots worming in between the
                              plasticine and chalk
Had changed your vision of our world?
What tip or cut had wrenched it out of joint
So that a broken crayon in a child's hand
Became a pillar of your temple crumbling down?

Buns for the Elephants

He'd never been right, they said,
Tapping their heads, but that
Zoo business was the end,
The straw-breaking-camel end.

That afternoon hot amber beads of bees
Had fussed in cliffs and caverns of blooms
Close under the open, air-teasing window.
His chalk voice scratched and died
With a small squeak on the blackboard
Of his soul, and Cardinal Wolsey's tussle
With Henry flaked to dust on his lips.
A curious silence and then Griffin,
Sniffing on the front row, slowly but
Definitely became a sleek, white doe.
Gittins next to him became a zebra, all the second
                                                                            row
Flamingos, Duffin with the stutter
A puffin, Birtles a turtle, the third
Row a knot of squirming crocodiles,
While four and five were lions and tigers.
Little Kelly, the baboon, grinned round the room,
Riley, the small Himalayan bear,
Sucked his pencil and dreamed of home-time,
And, one presumed, of honey and
                                          rhododendrons.

And as yet none of this new-sprung Form
Four Classical Zoo moved! They
Stared at him as though they cared!
As though they could listen all day
To tangled tales of Tudor turmoil!
Four tuskers on the back row swung
Their long trunks wisely, flapped their ears
And waited, and waited, and nodded and
                                                    waited.

The silence in the zoo grew, until
One of the crocodiles nudged the puffin,
Who winked at the baboon, who put his hand
Up and said, *Sir! Is something wrong?*

And then he saw it, right outside the door,
Where once had been a playground and a wall,
And buses and gardens and birdbaths and
                                                    shops,
The great plain of the Serengeti shimmered
Under the smelting sun. He saw
Giant baobab trees baboon-berried,
Weaverbirds knitting the branches
Together above the slowly stalking
Geometry of giraffes. He laughed, and all
The while, outside for a million miles or more,
The endless African sky waited.

Get out! he shouted, opening the door
To the heat and the booming roar
Of infinities of insects meshing their cogs.

Shoo! Shoo! and the blazered zoo
Trundled out into the puzzled playground
And hung about in an absurd confused herd.

Back! he said to the jungle. *Be free –*
For ever. Can we be friends? After all
I've done to you? Tomorrow meet me
At the forest's dwindling edge,
Where the great plains and the tree worlds meet
And the treacly river runs.
I will bring the elephants some buns.

The Bike

A month of mithering or so and you were mine.
For me you brought release. I never thought
That dancing wheels and spinning cranks,
As air clung round and pulled me up
Far hills that I had only seen before
In hazy distance from our street end, could
Carry me so far from that stone maze
And up on to the moor top. There I looked
Back down at all my Sunday world
Spread out below the hills,
The stubble of chimneys and the mills,
Church steeples, chapel roofs and schools. Then I,
Amongst the heather, was as far
From home as any stranger to the world
And only had to turn my back this once, just
                                            once
And cross those far crags and those further
                                            lonely hills,
That cloud-capped fell, to be
Perhaps for ever free – until I
Heard the others ring their bells and knew that
                                            we
Would be late home for church and tea.

mithering: worrying, moaning

The Dump

Across the tip we played,
Where summers ran screaming
On schooldays-end legs
And cogwheels gnawed the cinder path
With hungry teeth of rust. It was there that
Gantries looped their smashed arms gone awry
And toppled into pools of ebony oil,
Where cables hissed and slithered in the wind.

All those hot summer days of childhood
The tip smelt of oil and rust and grass.
Great boilers boomed like stranded whales,
Their skin a dry, red, crispy shingle
That burst into a flame of copper moths
Beneath the bricks we threw.

Then we left them to their dying;
Watched the birds nest in their clutches,
Those cast-off old machines that grabbed the sky.
The fireweed and the ragwort made their way
Through spokes and ducts and sumps
And flashed green rags of banners in the sun.

My playground was a tip,
My countryside a waste of brick and dust,
Where grass and rain gnawed, picked and bit
As the slowly changing landscape fell to rust.

gantry: a bridge-like structure supporting a crane
sump: pit or well

Bobby Swings

Jump! they said. *Jump!* and I looked at the ground
Below the cliff and the great tree high above
Where his hands clutched the rope.
You're scared, they gibed and he swung and
                                          slithered off,
Scraping slowly down the quarryside, as flowers
                                                   of blood
Spread gently across his face like stolen jam.
Ripening, raw leaves of skin the cliff had torn
Hung limp and his scream was like
The wail of the dog the trolleybus once hit.

Within a week he swung again
And made the other side,
In bandages and plaster, a crazed white ape
Who banished the word 'scared'.

Years later in a city pub I heard the news.
One night the lads had dared him and he'd done
A ton plus on his motor bike, pointed
It down that dark road to the stars,
Burning the rubber, feeling the earth spin away,
The battering air gibbering about his ears.
He lost it on the bend, sailed head on into that
Old swinging tree; no second chance
For Bobby now to swing across the spinning
                                                          years.

The Road to Beyond

The Son of the King of Nowhere

When Felix the Tinker came to town
And threw down his shovel money on the
                                        counter
Ears went up and eyes looked out
When the Son of the King of Nowhere shouted:

A large Black Bush and a pint of Guinness
And one of your meat and potato pies, missis
And have a drink yourself. That's grand. Cheers!
Here's health! 'Slainte and farewell to care!'
Is the call of the Son of the King of Nowhere.

And the music started and Felix danced
His lunging, lurking, staggering dance,
Stopping wall-eyed and sweating,
Face burning, staring into the air.
So who wants to fight? I'll part his hair!
He'll be sorry he met the Son of the King of Nowhere.

But oh, Felix, when the lights were out in the
        snug
And the dog sleeping on the rug
And the porter rings drying on the unwiped
        copper,
You crawled away to your Winter Palace, that
        cold corner
In Rat Street and huddled up your tinker's
Dreams with the cold old moon rolling
On the rooftops.

And then you gave a curse for the world,
Coiled up like an old moggy cat in that bare
Room, lost and lonely, just you only,
Tinker prince, Son of the King of Nowhere. •

Black Bush: a brand of Irish whiskey
slainte: cheers

What of the Night?

What of the night,
Its lamp-black hand
Rubbing the town towards sleep,
The street-lamps scratching through
And the tracer flares of tail-lights
Snaking down the square,
Where winter trees bunch their knuckles
On a windy, lamp-jigging sky?

What of the night,
Where, in this city café,
A baby in a high chair
Bangs a spoon while, outside
Across the night sea of the sky, the moon scours
                                                        clouds
And on the street a lone fat lady peers
Up into space, her tongue moving across her
                                                         lips,
As the clouds sashay across the moon?

What of the night,
Where a man writes
Alone in the café,
Looking at the child, the fat lady, the sky
And silver-sixpence moon, and the winter's
                                                       night
Moving with infinite compassion
Through the frost-spangled town?

Lucky Legs

In a one-bulb room in a one-way street
He opened up his eyes,
He saw the pale light in the gloom,
His mother heard him cry;
In a one-chance town on a luckless day
To the howl of a passing train
While outside the posters in the street
Were peeling in the rain.

In streets along the dockyard wall
He learnt the creed of the city:
Dog eat cat, don't turn your back,
Grab and take and show no pity;
Despise the weak, never show the other cheek,
Don't let weakness drag you down.
Con men and crooks your only books,
Swim and let the others drown.

And as he grew to man's estate,
Lucky Legs made his mark;
Sleek and black as an alley cat,
He was King of the Dark.
His face grew scars like exploding stars,
His only lover a gun;
In the dawn of the day he hid away
From the cruel light of the sun.

And Lucky Legs they called him then
As down the nights he ran,
A tearaway afraid of the day,
But he was a drowning man.
A small-time strutting midden cock
Who didn't know the day was late,
While around him in the darker dark
The foxes lay in wait.

In a one-way street in a no-chance town,
A shotgun found its mark
And took him apart like a rain of knives
Just on the edge of dark;
Only the death of a small-time loser,
His mother heard his scream of pain
While the posters in the city streets
Were peeling in the rain.

Jimmy Spoons

Down the long city streets on summer afternoons
There walked an old man, they called him Jimmy Spoons.
There were times that I remember, me and all the other kids,
How we followed him the long, long day through.

Singing, *Hey, Jimmy, won't you play one more tune,*
One of those you learnt across in France?
Hey, Jimmy, won't you play just one more,
Play one so the little kids can dance?

He played his old mouth-organ and his spoons they beat out time,
All the kids they followed him, he didn't seem to mind.
Lots of times I often wondered why he was just a tramp

And where he went when the long hot days
                                        were done.

All his ribboned medals they spangled in the
                                                     sun,
Memories of the trenches and a hell that was
                                        long gone.
But now he was no soldier, just a dosser out of
                                                 luck,
Living in that hostel on the hill.

Somewhere out in France a shell had torn his
                                                mind,
Left him burnt and broken, wearing rags,
                                        wearing a smile.
What happened in those trenches, in the
                              screaming mud and tears,
What happened to your life, Jimmy Spoons?

Down the long city streets I walk past my old
                                                home,
I've seen some changes, now that I have grown.
Yet still the kids come running on a summer's
                                              afternoon
And you hear them all call out to Jimmy Spoons.

Hey, Jimmy, won't you play one more tune,
One of those you learnt across in France?
Hey, Jimmy, won't you give us just one more,
Play one so the little kids can dance,
Play one so the little kids can dance?

The Sally-dosser Man

We gave him tea, my mam and gran and me,
When he came with his stale cake and old dry
butties.
But we made him eat them, drink it on the
garden wall.

Not in the house, his feet are wet, said my mam,
Not in the house, or it's cheeky he'll get, said my
                                                gran.
So it's not in our house, nor nobody's house, but
                                            the wall –
For the Sally-dosser man.

I remember once he gave me some of his old
                                        fruit-cake
And stale, shop-leaving sandwiches,
All wrapped and bundled in yesteryear's news,
Unfolding like flowers in his sea-veined hands,
Dry as the deserts of streets he'd crossed,
Hard as the stares from curtained windows.

And skipping children mocked him down the
                                            street
Shouting, *Tramp! Tramp! Paraffin lamp!*
I remember too, me high as his rope belt,
Stood watching from the door; and him,
String-held-tatter man, moving-on man,
Shop-back-dustbin man, Sally-dosser man,
Walking on fly's-eye cobbles, mirrored with rain,
Leaving a sucked-empty teacup
On the garden wall.

sally-dosser: a tramp or homeless person, who slept –
  'dossed' – at the Salvation Army hostels

Sheffield With Roses

A warren of mean streets, the station left
Behind, rolled past us, clicked like frames of
                                            film.
One row, long, red, dull brick and dim
Ran with the train along the tracks
As we pulled slowly out. The yards,
Bin full, with pale, dim huddles of wet rags,
Bald mops and worn sandstones. House after
                                                house
Rolled by till one, just one house in the row
Alone was a burst, a carnival
Of colour and roses, roses, everywhere
Were spattered all about that yard.

From old paint tins and buckets, old pot sinks
And slopstones rose-trees grew
And filled the yard, crawled out across
The broken pigeon loft and rambled round
The door where one old man stood on his step,
Shaded his eyes against our windowed sun
And watched the train and people passing by
His life. And he alone stood in a fire,
A hosanna, a benediction, a pentecost
Of wind-twitched roses, summer-burning
In a waste of brick and slate and soot and slag.

Train by Skerries

The Mourne Mountains a blue crinkle in the haze
Our train flickered by, running a dog along the
Railings, its shadow barking after us.
Children on the beach waved and one, just one
                              jumped,
Folding her legs under her, suspended in my
                              mind for ever,
Hair streaming goodbye as she shot behind a
                              Martello tower.
Beside me a nun reading and a priest reading
And the feeling that there was an ending and
                              beginning,
Here in all meeting, the child hung on a moment
And the eternal sea falling on the shore was all
And the child still hung upon the air was all
And the broom, burning in the late May sun was
                              all, was all.

Merman

The seaweed did it – got caught up,
Knackered, struggling like a seal pup,
When of a sudden the perfidious sea
Spewed me into the net.
What a morning whoop and holler there was!
Prod and pinch and kick and carry,
Stone cell-flags and them all peering
Calling in their gibberish through the bars
And a man in black, a cross in one hand
Chucking holy water with the other.
They put me in a creek for fear I would die
Before the freak-show master came;
Iron staves and net to fence me in
And children moon-eyed, mud-faced
Stared, squeaking shrill and nudging through
                                               the fence.

Two men on watch with a bottle and their pipes,
The moon rose over the headland and one swipe
Of my tail beneath the sleeping boozers' noses
And I was out to sea under a harvest moon,
Leaving behind only a trail of phosphorescence,
A carving on a tympanum
And a stack of winter's tales.

Mapmaking

Alphabet

Twenty-six flowers.
Oh, what a web of tales!
What worlds, what golden truths!
What leaden lies!
What walls they build, what castles
And what dungeons.
Twenty-six flying birds,
Who knows how they fly
Or where they land?

Village Wedding

I climbed through mist into a gully in the crags
Cleft and, once up and through, the hags
Ran silver in the suck of peat and sudden
Sheep bucked and ran the beck.

A world of sodden white, cold by the Bride
Stones ledge I turned and took the line
Of wall that falls towards the sour moor and
The smoke-black gritstone chapel on its edge.

Sliding fishlike out of the cloud I scrambled
Over peat and heather and rambled to the lane
And saw them frozen in the lich-gate, a crowd
Of smiles held in a sudden spillage of spring sun.

Veiled like a nun she smiled out at the lens,
Stood by the fire-faced, dazzled boy
Who somehow sensed the day was given now
To something older and beyond.

Nose-picking bridesmaids were nudged in place
By an aunt, all hat and handbag and new shoes,
And another lick of sun washed them
As the shutter clicked again for sideboard frames

And albums and the stares of years to come.
*Oh, look at Gran! That lovely dress. At least you had
the sun.*
And they'll see the men uncomfortable in suits,
The anxious farmer uncles thinking of the pub

And looking at the flowers and dresses, they'll
see,
Perhaps, behind the church the Bride Stones flame
That have seen three thousand years and more
Of such beginnings, such sun-blessed wedding
days.

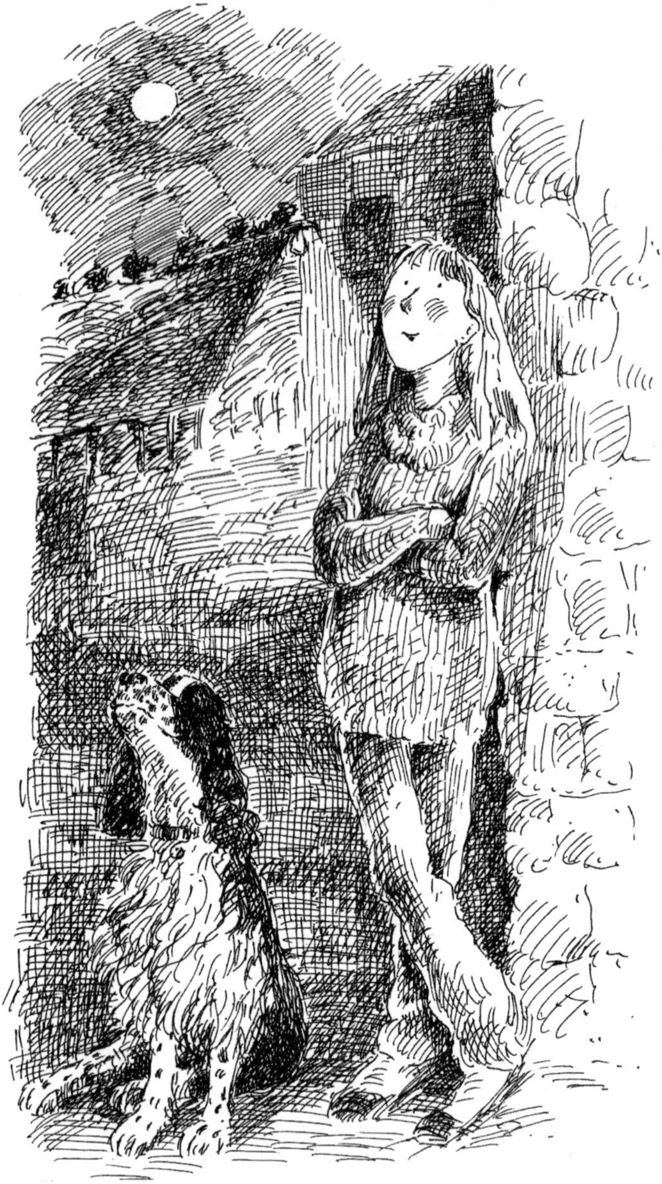

After the Wedding

Honeymoon gone she'll stand on silent nights
Watching her breath steam in the cold yard-light
As falling stars scratch the lamp-black sky
And by the stove, lapped in sacks, dry
And warm, a coddled, sick lamb breathes
Soft milky bubbles on the rug,
And she sees the years ahead stretch further
And more curious than the questioning stars.

Wind and the Angries

I throw back the curtains
And let the grey-green light in,
But the wind plays rock and roll about the house.

I tidy away last night's supper things
And wrap my dressing-gown tighter,
But the wind plays rock and roll about the house.

I sit with my bowl of breakfast
And try to ignore the racket,
But the wind plays rock and roll about the house.

For the fire hums in tune
And the windows tap out the rhythm
As the wind plays rock and roll about the house.

Above the string quartets
Of men's little bitty houses,
The wind plays the hill like a guitar,
Picking unimaginable notes out of the fretwork
                                  of the crags.
Tempest, the drummer in wind's group has
                                  picked up trees,
And with them he is playing
Paradiddles on the timpani of the fell.

Gusty, the mad saxman, is hitting top B flat,
Bebopping through the scars.
Sheep lurk against the walls
Putting their horns in their ears
And Howl, the singer in Wind and the Angries

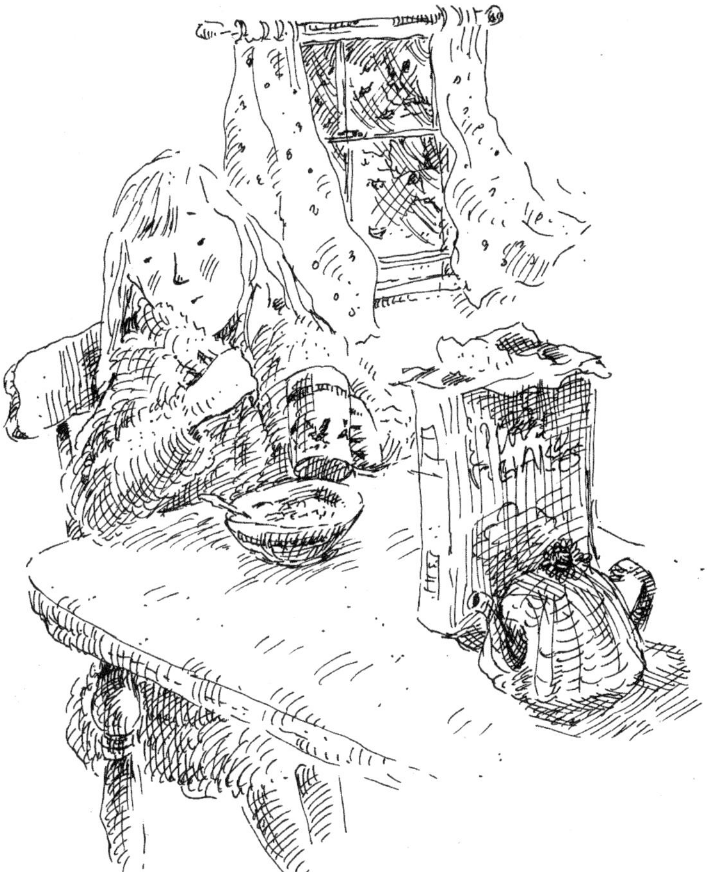

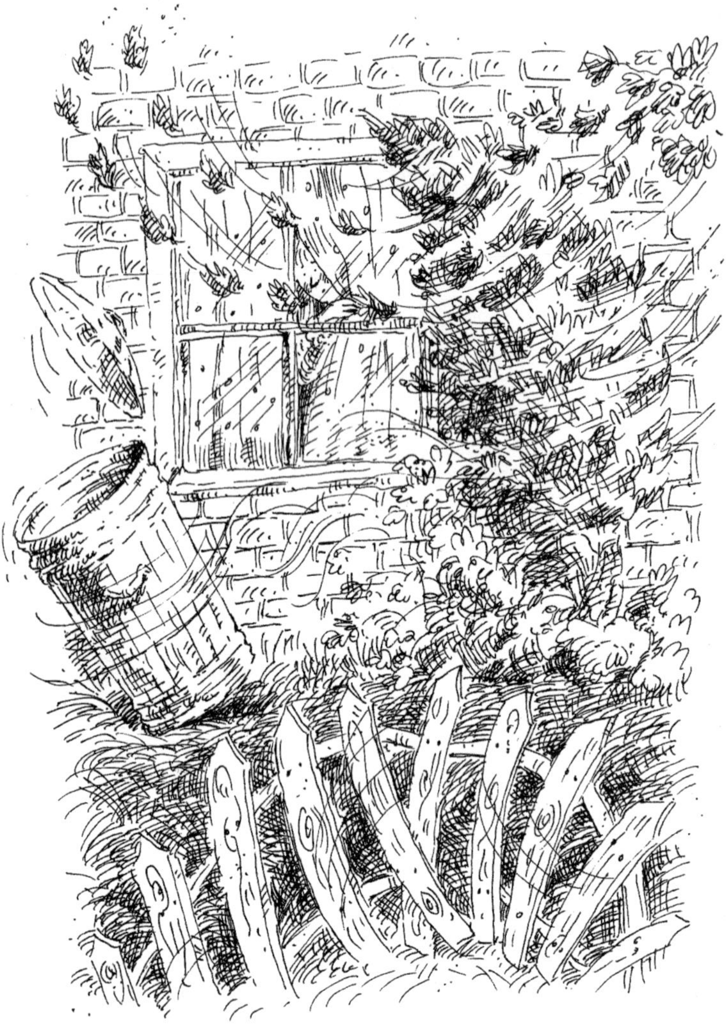

Is screaming out the words to his song
Through the million megawatt amp of the hills,
AIEEESHOOORWHAAAAA!
                        AIEEESHOOORWHAAAAA!
RRRROOOOOFAFAFAFAFA!
                        RRRROOOOOFAFAFAFAFAFA!
Over the tiny, silly, rumba-ing roofs of men.

And the hills are bopping,
The trees boogaloo, the railings rap,
The fences sashay and the dustbins roll around,
Breakdancing on the shaking ground.
The bushes conga and the shrubs rumba
And a fine old fandango goes on all around.
Oh, the wind is playing rock and roll around the
                                                house
And I, though I pretend I'm not,
Am very, very, very scared
When the wind plays rock and roll around the
                                                house.

The Song of the Flute

Blow a breath into me, man; lip to ebony lip,
Make the quick air thicken, pulse and thrum.
Tip and swirl the song, your fingers flickering
                                              up
My spine and let reel round the room

My throbbing soul of wood. From root to branch,
                                              core
To twig, from heart to arm to wrist to finger's
                                              cran,
All song, and breath, and wind, his bigger
                                              brother,
Shouting in the branches, howling off the land

And battering the soft heads of the waves.
And the set dancers on the harbour flags twist
And wind to the tune's tickle and shout. Man,
                                              chance
A swirl of wood-song, tap-root dance.

Such a small stick in the hollow of your hand,
Come lip to lip and let us, lovers, kiss.

cran: a fingering technique for grace-notes on the flute

The Heroic Clouds

The heroic clouds like boxers roll
Out of the harrying of the west and sashay
Over the crag. They clinch, bunch, maul
And butt, muttering thunder threats under
Their breath before they fling themselves
Into the ring.

Cowards! They gang up together and jump
The falling sun, kidney punching, head butting,
Hitting him when he's down.
No gong saves him – he's gone.
And the heroic clouds, their shirt-tails bloody
                                      and brass,
Hold their hands above their heads
And their swaggering, bullyboy roars of
                                      triumph
Shake the windows all along the dale.

Curtains

The way he drew the curtains irked you so,
His magazines left on the seats of chairs,
His bubbling pipe, the broken mouse-turd trail
Of dried hard mud from his boots up the stairs,

His cough before he spoke and those old lines:
Well, worse things happen at sea! Fair dos!
And *Cheer up, you're a long time dead!*
But now as you Oxfam his clothes and shoes,

Those Christmas ties he never wore,
And bin his 'comics' and his tarry pipes,
What would you give to find those shards of
                                                mud,
The morning curtains hanging 'just not right',

A chip of cough from somewhere in the house
Before, *Love, have you seen my . . . ?*

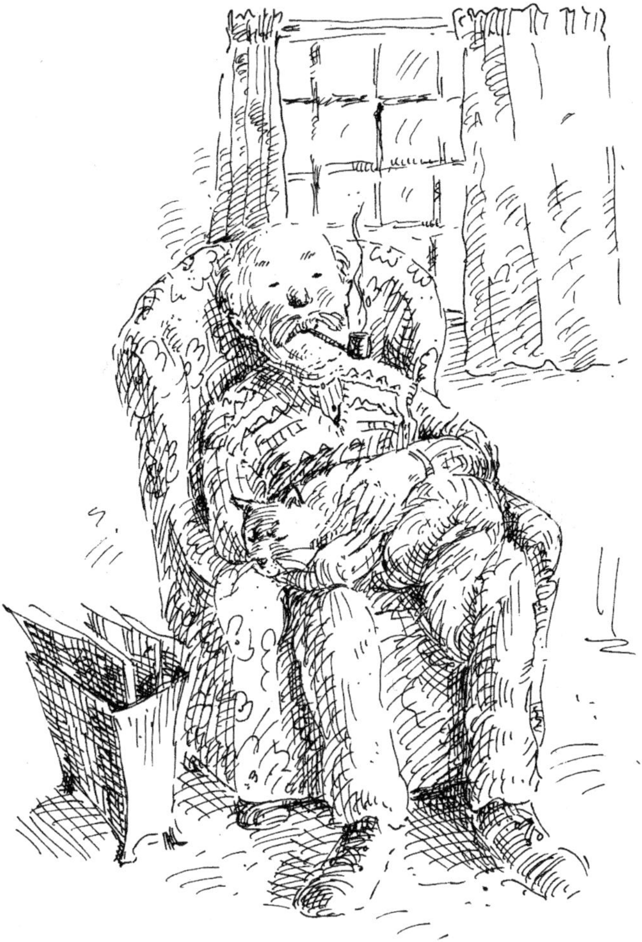

Swallows

The swallows are putting the deckchairs away,
Laying a tarpaulin over the land,
Gathering, dotted crotchets on the wires.
Passing, I sight-read 'The Last Rose of Summer'.

Then they are in the air, 'chucking' in agreement,
Trying out their wings over Rottenbutts Wood,
Where leaves are trimmed with a pale tint
Of rust, this season's newest fashion.

The swallows muster all along the dale,
Clot, swarm and cluster,
Scenting warm seas and brass-bright desert
                                                      skies,
Hearing a murmur of Africa on a Dales' wind.

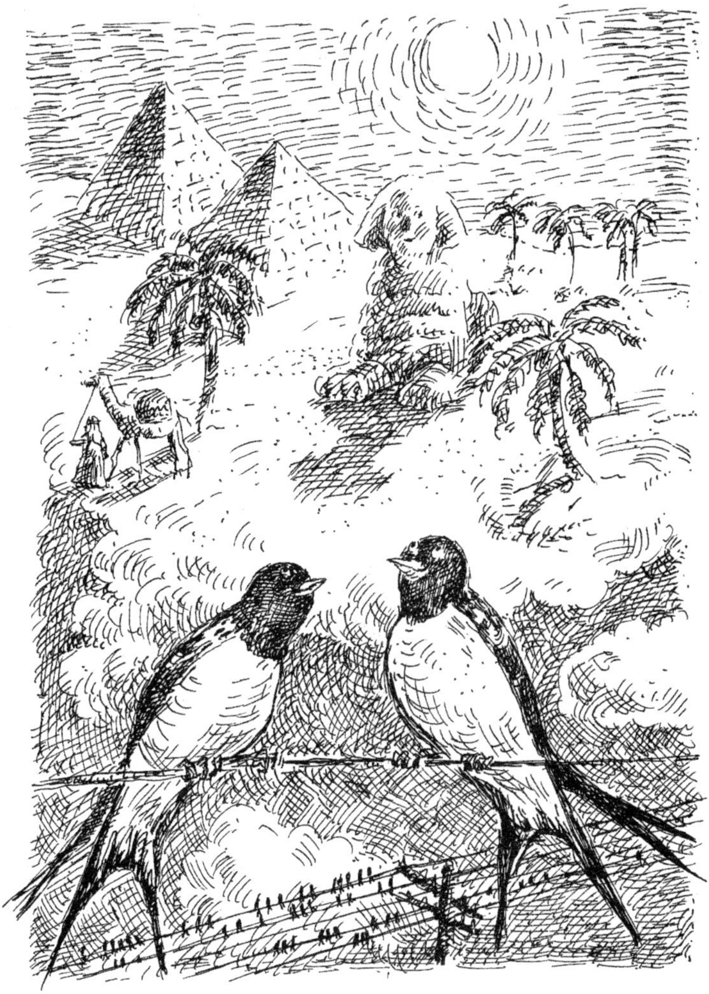

Autumn Dentdale

Year calling *Time*, beating brass gongs,
Chucks summer out and hammers up a wind.
And all the trees turn fires and precious stones,
Are tiger's-eyes, cornelian, jasper and topaz.
Leaves leap, tin fish they rust and swim from
                                              trees,
Tumbled in the currents of the carousel winds.
Falling, the fire flakes lig, clumped
In cuprous swirls and dunes to rot.

The Year's litter-lout turns out, he breezes
In the wood and rips the wrappers off the trees
To toss them on the grass. In gutter they glitter,
On the beck sumped below the drumming falls

They sinter, and clinker skims the crucible of the
                                                pool;
Whirling dross, molten ore, fool's gold,
Parrot's feathers, lemons and oranges,
Egg-yolk, clown's nose, pips from the sun.

chucks: throws
lig: lie
cuprous: coppery
sinter: turn into rock

Lune Sun

Look! said the father,
Hoisting his child on the wall,
*The sun on the Lune is a balloon,
And look! The heron on the mud
Tucks its head beneath its wings.*

*Look how the bird flies now,
Look at the brassy-faced sun,
Look at the river, how still and breath-unruffled,
Look how the river is a mirror,
Look! Look!*

And the child, his daughter,
Said, *Look, Dad, that's us
In the water! Look!*

Diggers

They came and sliced the turf from off
Dub Hill with surgeons' care, then peeled
It from the skull and laid bare brown,
Clay barrow rings, stone chambers, sunk
Cyst walls. For months after, they came
And scraped and brushed and sliced and took
Back shards and iron slag and yellow
Brittle bones.

A field away Jack Sedgwick keeps
His yowes for tupping. Jack, whose blood
First beat here in the barrow wrights,
Whose bones come from a mould laid down
When ice began to melt. Across
The field he watched them in the sun
Dig up his people's grave beneath
The standing stones.

yowes: sheep
tupping: mating

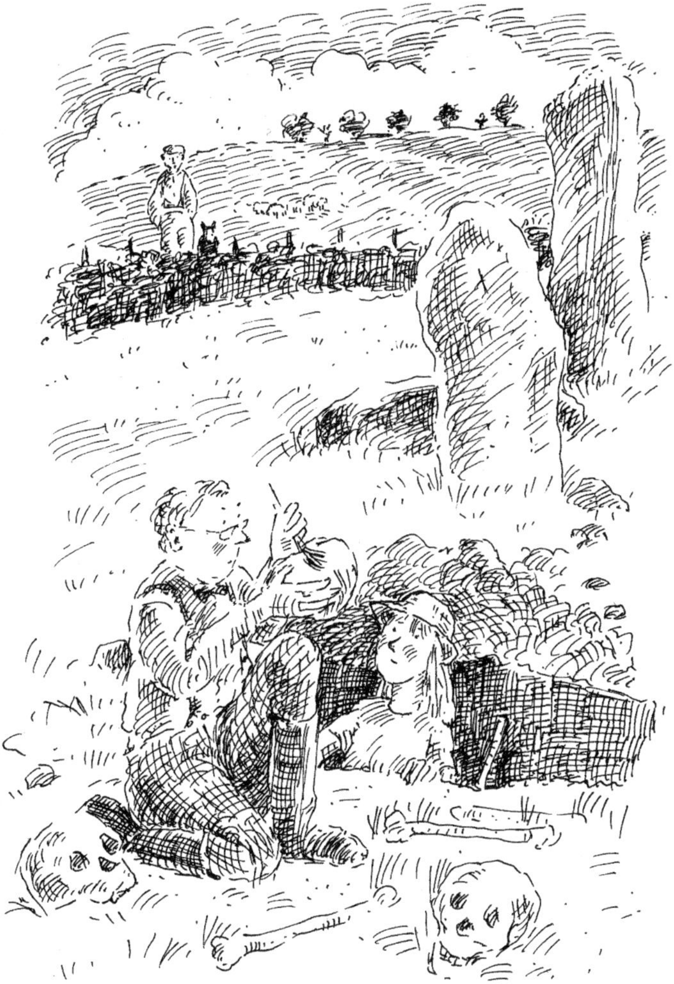

Mapmakers

With line and spyglass and thread
The red-coated men made a book of the land,
Plumb and angle and square and set.
Named points, gills, rocks, beacons, spanned
Marshes and laid open the fast
Hides of rebels.

Knowing my name you know me,
Naming my land you own me.
Land cast and cusped before
Only in tongue and mind
Now stamped in lead on a chart
For strangers' eyes to read.

They made a page of the fell,
Hauled stone over bog and scree,
Mashed mortar with bog water
And by the secret mounds of buried kings
Whose cairns looked to the west
They set their bronze-capped column
To fix the shifting land.

Paper Boats

Each poem a fold of words
Nip and tuck,
One more for luck;
Crease the prow of rhyme, each sheet
A sail of beaten sound,
Each mast a clutch of hammered images.

Out on the pond now,
Sink or swim,
One last snip – perhaps?

There they go, bobbing up and down:
Sonnet tugboats,
Galleons of ballads,
And little tubby twelve-line smacks and luggers,
All scattered by the wind, to make landfall where?

Index of First Lines

A day it is that fingers its way	15
A month of mithering or so and you were mine	37
A warren of mean streets, the station left	52
Across the tip we played	38
Blow a breath into me, man; lip to ebony lip	66
Down the long city streets on summer afternoons	48
Each poem a fold of words	77
Every Sunday in summer he came in his van	26
Give in! your classmates said. *Give in!* – sharing	30
Had a cat, Mushycat	18
He'd never been right, they said	34
Honeymoon gone she'll stand on silent nights	61
I climbed through mist into a gully in the crags	58
I saw them as I lay beside the pools	16
I throw back the curtains	62
I was up in the morning with nothing to do	13
In a desk he is caged	28
In a one-bulb room in a one-way street	46
Jump! they said. *Jump!* and I looked at the ground	39
Look! said the father	73
My grandfather played a fiddle	24
Tall, white-haired in her widow's black	23

The frost curled fat fine flowers of ice about	22
The heroic clouds like boxers roll	67
The Mourne Mountains a blue crinkle in the haze	53
The seaweed did it – got caught up	54
The swallows are putting the deckchairs away	70
The way he drew the curtains irked you so	68
There was no walking then, only running	20
They came and sliced the turf from off	74
Twenty-six flowers	57
We gave him tea, my mam and gran and me	50
What of the night	45
When Felix the Tinker came to town	43
With line and spyglass and thread	76
Year calling *Time*, beating brass gongs	72
Your screaming sent the spiders to their holes	32